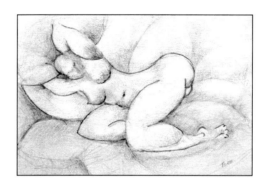

Dirty Secrets

Theo Sable

Library of Congress Control Number: 2012921286
ISBN: Hardcover   978-1-4797-4837-2
                   Softcover   978-1-4797-4836-5
                   Ebook   978-1-4797-4838-9

This book was printed in the United States of America.

Illustrations by Theo

To order additional copies of this book, contact:
Xlibris Corporation
1-888-795-4274
www.Xlibris.com
Orders@Xlibris.com
123659

Contents

RELATIONSHIPS

POLITICS AND SOCIAL COMMENTARY

DEATH AND DECELERATION

A LITTLE LEVITY

METAPHYSICAL MUSINGS

TRUE LOVE

Dedication

For Jesse

Acknowledgment

I thank Mike Ross, a most gifted teacher at The North Carolina Center For Creative Retirement, and the talented students in his class, whose encouragement made all the difference. I also owe a tremendous debt of gratitude for her invaluable assistance to Perien Gray, a dear friend and poet of breathtaking honesty and skill. I am grateful to my children, Ben and Eric Monder, for their love and support, and to my husband, Jesse, who is both inspiration and reward.

Fame

My words, in type, take on a validity that they lack
When I am scribbling them in pencil
On the back of an envelope or on a yellow pad.
It's sad that even here, appearances count more than content
As I gaze on a rather sophomoric phrase,
Trying for a literary crown,
Relying on Arial black for posthumous renown.

PERSONAL

Memory

What did she teach me,
the little lady lately come from Poland,
mixing up her v's and w's
cooking up her superstitions with a soupçon of Parisian chic.
She laughed at the pretentious
while pretending to love motherhood:
a loyal wife who set her table with bitter condiments
before a silent man of action
who demanded to be served ahead of his only child.
Sitting across the vast maple tundra of misunderstandings,
wondering what I had done wrong again
I ate too fast.

Life Story

Beset by demons
My poor mother wept
No matter if I got good grades
Or ran in hallways
I tiptoed
Through my childhood
There are no recorded smiles
From my poor father's box camera.

As I grew sideways
Into puberty, avoiding all
The cracks between the paving stones
I fell into the first abyss
Presented by my captive circumstances
Married badly at nineteen
A tender age for anything
But most especially for contracts.

Night school was a revelation
As were annulments
Of all promises,
Aided by corrupt attorneys
And the stifled yawns of judges
Free again to stumble
Into ambiguity, seeking dreams.

If I awakened into daylight
I was still in my mother's nightmare
But I presently redeemed
Myself by marrying a Jewish doctor,
Whom I cunningly unearthed
In a TB sanatorium after
Cleverly disguising myself
As an ordinary patient.

Twenty years and two sons later
I emerged from my indentured
Wifedom, non the wiser, but much older
Still flat chested, but ambitious.

So I tried my hand at this and that
Whatever took was celebrated
And I managed to succeed
In modest fashion to survive.

Until one fateful business day
A noble Prince did come my way
While precious little did I know
Of magic spells and incantations
Somehow my life's preparations
Made me ready for the joust.

And I prevailed, and we made merry
Indeed we even made to marry
Still and into golden years
Together, demons on the losing side . . . .
It's too damn bad my mother died.

Too Smart
For My Own Good

They skipped me out of second grade
I don't know why.
My classroom was warm and sunny.
The desk was just my size.
I loved the smell of yellow paper from the wooden closet.
There were bright pictures on the walls and
the teacher smiled.

The next day I had to climb the concrete stairs
to the third floor.
The halls were long and dark.
My classroom's ceiling was very high.
The windows were so far up I couldn't see out and
they had cages on them.
The sun never came in.
Nobody smiled.

They skipped me out of second grade.
My mother was so proud.

The House is Small

The house is small, the street so narrow
It is hard to believe I was a child there
Where the boulevard seemed vast
Now is so shriveled, barely makes it to the corner.

It is hard to believe I was a child there
With reluctant steps I climbed the stairs
And now so shriveled I can barely make it to the corner
Gasping in the heavy air.

With uncertain steps I climb the stairs
Of newer houses, although I am old
Gasping in the heavy air
It is hard to believe I was a child.

What do you Want to be When you Grow Up?

My Godmother had a house in the country.
Well, to me it was the country. I lived with my parents
in a three room tenement flat in Brooklyn. She lived in a
house in Putnam County.

The only way to get there was by car.
You got to us by subway.
I shared the bedroom with my mother, who snored.
I got into the habit of sleeping with a pillow on my head.
I still do that, even though I'm the one who snores.

When I visited her house I had my own room!
The walls had flowered wallpaper; the ceiling slanted
romantically to the floor. The bed was a white four-poster
which had a ruffled coverlet and matching pillow cases.
When I went to bed I felt like a Princess.

There was a garden, there was a pond, there were trees all
around the house. The sun
Bathed the terrace at five o'clock, when my Godmother
would serve cocktails to her guests
And everyone said I was so smart and pretty
But the best ambition was of course to get married and have
children.

Back in Brooklyn, my mother was having none of that.
"Any cow can have a baby!" she would snort contemptuously.
"The best thing is to have a profession that no one can take
away from you!"
My mother climbed those four flights every day
With big bags of groceries.
She was always cooking, or cleaning or shopping.
It's amazing how much work you can find with just one child
and three rooms and a husband to take care of.
Full time occupation: housewife.
She hated it.

My Godmother had no children of her own.
She helped her husband in the department store they
owned.
She wore mauve nail polish and had very strong opinions.

What did I want to be when I grew up?

Guess.

No Place Like Home

Home
was no place
tribe of three,
Nomads of the Tenements, we moved
every year the first eight years of my life
to score the free
first three months of every lease (plus painting).
We settled down in Brooklyn for awhile and I sprouted roots
across the street from the Botanical Gardens,
that magical place that changed with the seasons. I could count
on the view to remain the same except for snow
that turned purple at dusk. I could count
on familial dysfunction any time of year so
I wrenched my life forward and outward and into
another place, only
worse.

Mother

I remember my drunken rant
In the wee hours of a weekday morning
Crying on the telephone not caring
If I woke you up not caring
That I cared too much and begging
You to please to please to please let go
My mother.
It took the alcohol and tears to tear
Us finally apart, our years umbilically entwined
Cut off my oxygen supply
I was convinced that I would die
In thrall to your desires for me.
It took Jim Beam and lots of ice to set me free.

The Cherry

We had a sundae late one Sunday afternoon
And ate it leisurely with just a single spoon
All soft and laughing, never mind the cost
A sudden lunge,
And more than love was lost.
With one fell swoop he pounced upon his prey!
It is not forgiven, even 'til this day . . .

Oh harbinger of things to come
Our union was at once and for all time, undone!

Thespian

I trade bright sunlight and fresh air
For murky and dark spaces, places where we read and lose
our places
From papers, underlined with need. I don't concede
That one is better than the other.

Lying through and around my teeth
I am forgiven the conceit of pretense if
Beneath my efforts to be clever
I am successful in the endeavor to convince
That I am someone other than who emerged from my
mother.

After the Divorce

I bought an apartment way downtown
You could go from room to room
That's it, just two but hey!
My half bought me Soho chic
And that's no small potatoes in the Big Apple.

But I didn't want to be there. No,
Not while my lover lived
On the upper west side
In a one room studio with a loft
Aloft. Oh that precious loft
I could loft it over all humanity
When I was there, safe
Upon the magic mattress on the floor
There was no more that I could want
I haunted it even when
He was out of town, I'd get the key
And hang around and sleep on sheets
I had selected for him. Manly sheets
With grey stripes denoting great sophistication
With no obeisance to things frilly.
That would be silly.

Sculptor

Never so much effort as in kneading dough, needing
Though to totally transform the substance
Substrate syncopate rhythmic push
What was once so pliant as a pile of mush
Becomes recalcitrant resistance to the hand.
Understand I need assistance on this job
If I'm ever to transform in starts and fits
This blob into something recognizable
If not sizeable. Finally
There it stands (or sits)
A monument to its intrinsicality.
Was there ever any doubt
That this was how it was going to turn out?

I am Shrinking

I'm shrinking into my little apartment
On the fifth floor
I don't need more
To make me happy and content
As long as the rent and I remain stable
I am able to stay.
Hurray!

It is no sin
To draw one's expectations in
After all, it wasn't long ago, oh my!
I saw the pterodactyls fly
Right by my window
And the price for fame and glory
Was gory. Now I rest
Upon what laurels seem the best
To gather in. It is no sin to sit
And watch the sunrise overtake the sky.
In fact, it is so lovely I could cry.

Second Childhood

They're grown and gone
It's time I, too, was moving on
Uncharted ways
My days unscripted, I won't know
When I start out, just where I'll go.

I landed here
Amidst the toys of learning, and I fear
I've not the strength of intellect or mind
Not to be left behind

But I still try
Not to shame Momma or my Dad
By being bad, and do my sums
And although nothing comes
Of it, I think
Just on the brink of brilliance,

I'll be good. So please explain
Why is the pain of ignorance
So sharp. You'd think
I would be used, by now, to muddling through.
Isn't that what I have always done,
And do?

Flirt

By now I should have grown too wise
To seek redemption in a stranger's eyes.
By now I am who I've become, but still
There is a secret kind of thrill to seemingly fulfill
Another's fantasy. I will
Indulge this foolishness to my regret
But I haven't kicked the bucket yet.

CAT

I Am Cat

Of all the creatures on the earth, I
have come to be with you,
to be your company
and let you know not everybody
walks on two, some run on four legs
and do not shave them, and I leave
big fluffy clumps of me in corners
to remind you that I am present even when
I sleep amidst your shoes in secret places
only your closet knows.

I may leap to catch the slightest morsel that you throw
to amuse me, but did you know
I only leap to amuse you?

Ode to My Cat

Oh, let me put my head against your furry side
and hide.
All strife and the vicissitudes of life
Will disappear when you are near
But I fear some urgent call will take you.
You just won't stay right here, and I can't make you!

Purring Poultice

Like a purring poultice replete with paws
he climbs on my belly and sheathes his claws.
I get a reassuring pat
and he is gone, and that is that
(what more can you ask from a black and white cat?).

Bandito

Our cat's name is Bandito; it suits him quite well
He wears a tuxedo and looks like a swell
Not stuck up or haughty, just devil may care
Surreptitiously naughty, but with savoir faire.

His favorite foods are whatever we eat
And when we are eating, he's under our feet!
His paw on my arm, his manners are lofty
He uses his charm, and he knows I'm a softy.

Yes, his best vacation would be on our table
Ingesting our rations whenever he's able
So set a new place for our little Tuxedo
And we'll toast the holidays with our Bandito!

purrfection

so it all comes down to this
sitting in sunlight and stroking my cat
humble recipient of his beneficence
honored with hand nuzzles
I am content
and if I could
I'd purr.

RELATIONSHIPS

Ode to Friendship

(I'm not complaining)
But where did it go, adrift
On multiple infractions
Actions that could be construed
As rude. I miss you
And the many confidences that we shared
We bared our adolescent souls to one another
When we dared. But now, in our maturity
We've opted for security, and so we go
Our separate ways, never again to know
The liberating joy of full confession
To a friend, and settle for a psychiatric session.

Erstwhile lover

Erstwhile lover
Purveyor of false charm
Imprisoned in my fears, I made your arms
the scaffolding of my distress
oh yes, and the escape route from my ancient pain.
How could I know, especially if I refused to look,
That you were craftily inventing such imaginative new
torments
That the old ones took on a nostalgic tinge when I
remembered them
Of course, that wasn't often
Your demands upon my time and consciousness precluded
reverie.
Oh erstwhile lover
You might have been the perfect man for me
If the wellsprings of good will had not withered in your
caustic wit
If the friends you banished from my life were worthless
If the deepest voices didn't have an evil overtone.
If I finally climbed out and was not welcome in the world.

His Briefcase

It boasted years of use. The lock didn't work any more
The tongue futilely flapped against the catch
The secrets kept inside available to any stranger.

The marriage didn't work any more,
but he was a catch, a doctor.
It would take more than biochemistry
(try alchemy)
To keep the secrets still inside while we were each
Available to any stranger.

There is a chic nobility to outworn leather
Cracked in places, with the shiny newness gone.
Not so the outworn empty wedding vows
Demanding to be filled with anything but this!

Some things

Some things
are better left unsaid.
After you're dead it's much too late
to set the record straight, but sometimes,
sometimes, misunderstandings are the key
to undisturbed tranquility.
Sometimes it's better to believe a total lie
Than to know the bitter truth and cry.

With Friends Like These

Enchanting, prancing
over his obligations, glancing
over his furry shoulder
like an effete gazelle, he smiles
his dimpled smile and reassures.
The consummate con man endures
For yet another season
With limitless reserves of charm. What harm
Is there in kissing yet another hand?
It's simply grand to watch his effortless technique
One must ignore the transient fits of pique,
Occasional absences without an explanation
Doubtless a vacation from his day job of a life.
His wife has no idea just where he's been,
For neither man nor beast, he won't come clean

Dirty Secrets

A surreptitious smirk
might work, where a fulsome smile
would not beguile. I swear
I'm glad I wasn't there to see
The fumbling furtive fucking in the dark
The amorous analogies to necking in the park
The panting panty raid, the unzipped fly
don't even want to try imagining, not I,
the fly upon the wall.
No, not at all. I'd rather bask in ignorance of shame
(Not sure they even knew each other's name.)

Scuttlebut

Stab me, and I'll crawl like a bug on the wall
Just outside, not to bleed on your rug.
If I were something furry, don't worry, I'd scurry
I won't be much trouble; I'm small.

If you make me a place
I'd erase myself truly, and not be unduly assertive.
I'd sit and I'd munch on the crumbs of your lunch
If I couldn't be fit, I'd be furtive.

If my humble effacement offends you
Displacement is often the way people cope.
For I'm nothing but chattel, you treat me like cattle
To be yanked at the end of your rope.

You do me a disservice if you think I am nervous
About my subservient role
If no pain, there's no gain and I'd stand in the rain
And relinquish my unworthy soul

For a glance, for a smile, I shall expire in style
At your feet as you step from your carriage
For the error was mine, I mistook the divine
For the hellish thing that is our marriaqe.

A Do-Over

Why
after all these years is he still here
spoiling
For a fight spoiling
my night showing up uninvited
in otherwise bucolic dreamscapes.

I don't know
what more I have to do! Divorce,
apparently, was not enough, nor thirty years
of blissful independence of his scorn
nor even death (oh yes, he died)
can rid me of his malignant presence. I do swear
it's a do-over. You know,
like in a game when you have made the wrong move
and you want to start again.
Like waking up next to a stranger,
wearing matching wedding bands.

You know,
the usual.

Who Are These People?

Who are these people?
Amalgamations of marital mistakes
Crowd my nights and make the early waking welcome.
Welcome to my phantom world of conversations with the
dead.
Reincarnations that I dread revolve around
Recriminations and the things unsaid
Which must be worse than anything we might have done.
It's just no fun to dream and in the night
There's no safe place to run.

I Can't Be Cured By Courtesy

I can't be cured by courtesy.
The illness of my life, too long endured
To then be cured by correct forms
And proper invitations to partake of polite conversations
While I ache to scream my hunger at the tea cups and the tea.
But fantasy does well for me.
I rarely find the comfort or the care in any place
But where I put myself, amidst companions of my mind,
Who shower me with compliments, are kind,
And never fail in their devotions
To the innate superiority of my emotions.
Yes, dreams are best.
As long as you do not intrude upon my carefully well-peopled solitude
I'll manage, but if you should ask me for a dance, and hum the tune,
And while the orchestra still plays and I want more, you go too soon
And leave me swaying in the middle of the floor,
Don't be surprised to find the moment charged with light and danger
And yourself confronted by a total stranger.

POLITICS
AND SOCIAL
COMMENTARY

Greed

Is there an antidote for avarice?
Can one do good works without the perks?
I used to think it was testosterone that would do us in
But no, it's an underrated sin
That's filling up the gulf of our insatiable desire.
Not celestial fire, nor brimstone, nor even evil circumstances
That are limiting our chances. It is greed
In all its manly manifestations:
Not race relations, nor the wicked seed;
Just the need for more than what you need.
Just greed.

The dinosaurs are having their last laugh
For it is they who write our final epitaph.
No use to fill a time capsule for future generations to
unearth.
The roaches won't know what we lost, nor care what it was
worth.

Versailles

Versailles had many rooms,
quite opulent, abundant, but
the ballroom was the biggest
certainly the brightest
mirrored on all sides and ceiling
foolishly festooned with frothy furbelows
to entertain the nobles.

The peasantry below,
remark on how resplendent royalty cavorts
in courtliest quadrilles. They cheer
in affirmation of their inferior status,
tithing, ever tithing hard earned sous to those above them.

Onward spins the mirrored ball,
the glitter and the make-believe, the lure of empty
promises,
the hint of hidden laughter from the room beyond.
They charm us, winking to each other,
and laying down our birthright like a cape to keep their feet
dry
we bade them walk upon us
to our everlasting shame.

Excremental Increments

In excremental increments
Our political scene is getting meaner,
The crowd, louder;
The sense, denser.
Nonsensical attacks are met with lax
Speculation or with scant regard
And it is hard to watch this dire unmaking
Of our democratic undertaking. Indeed
Undertakers are what we will need
If we fight back the oligarchic creed
That rules this once free land.
If we disband adherence to peaceful demonstrations
The weapons in the hands of other nations
Will quell us
Or so they tell us.

Perhaps our only recourse is to strike!
Just stop. Whatever we are doing
Whether working hard or wooing
Hunting, gathering, adding or subtracting,
Any acting is a crime if it is done to profit
Those who hide behind corrupted laws
The beasts with greedy paws are now in charge.
How long will we allow them to remain at large?

Carnivore's Lament

He died at dinner: to
Exsanguinate upon one's plate
Seems only fitting. At one sitting
One can consume the carcasses of many species
And one's feces don't discriminate among them
Whether you have shot or hung them
They are dead, and at your door.
Need I say more?

The 99%

The dandelion daisies were cut down before their time
Let that be a lesson to the raffish rest of us,
Ill bred unpedigreed upstarts garnishing the garden
With unwanted mutant spores. We cling
To the precipice and other habitats where only
The most tenacious tendrils hold to the untenable
And to opinions likewise sprung from an unlikely spring.

If we were watered daily, seeded, spread, our vines
Grafted to aristocratic saplings, we might flourish
In the sunlight of unfettered meadows, but
The gnarly ground the thatch the grievous soil
To which we most were born bears no resemblance to
The pastures of the rich.
We lick the drops the Calla Lilly leaves
We wilt
We die.

Too many tears
for a tissue

I watched the black ant carry, at right angles to his head,
a fallen brother, across my wide wooden floor
no doubt the victim of my impatient stamp
when I was (in my haste to get to breakfast)
too lazy to pick him up and throw the interloper out of doors
into his own domain and out of mine. But there they were
victim and rescuer making painful progress
towards some first aid station behind enemy lines
and I, to add fatal injury to insult, trying to pick them up
only succeeded in separating the two and finally
finishing the one.

My remorse is overwhelming and I'm left to wonder
why we humans are so inclined to ignore our fallen,
blaming them for their own misfortunes
not even picking up with toilet tissue
the lives we shatter with our own indifference.

was politics a dirty word

was politics a dirty word
when Plato sat; or Aristotle
surrounded by ideas full throttle
giving to Athenian youth
the Truth

when did it become calumny
and infamous deceit
to lie your way to powerful places
inflame the races
and line your pockets with the spoils of the elite?

Humanity may dumb its way to death: the earth will spin
Regardless of the tribes that did it in

It's a Boy!!!!!

Mindless Maleness
ejaculating bullets and reloading
the stench of death
accompanies the screams

the disbelievers
finally convinced that worship becomes war
as women see their children fall
slide into their own blood

guilty humankind will not give up
it's guns the carnage spreads. Too bad
the state is more concerned
with voter fraud.

A Handmaiden

A handmaiden to the basketmakers who provide
what we are all going to hell in
is hardly the authority on righteous living.

I'm just giving an opinion, which is worth
the price you paid for it, but
I wonder when the ignorant advise the uninformed
and the check on checks and balances
becomes too high a bill to pay,
out come the pseudo-patriots who were made for it.

One can only hope that the flag
in which they wrap themselves so tightly
constricts their circulation to the point of strangulation
for then and only then can we become a better nation.

Too High Strung

Too high strung for motherhood
The brotherhood of man was more my style.
You'd find me in the aisle of social justice
Or, for kicks, numismatics or magic tricks.
Perhaps chasing a lost cause inspired my invention,
Or enlightenment. Some good intention
Might have spurred me on, before
All my youthful energy was gone, but now
I linger over fearful headlines
And won't lift a finger.

DEATH
AND
DECELERATION

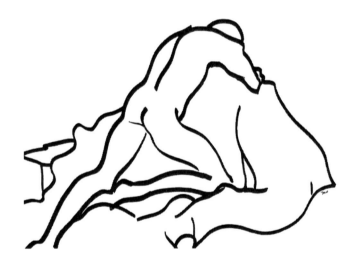

Attachments
and devices

Attachments and devices
are the price you pay
for living past your warranties.
Some brand new knees perhaps,
or even steel clad vertebrae
can save the day.

If you've attained your golden age,
I hear that hearing aids are all the rage
and for the very nearly blind
there is a kind of system that enlarges type:
they also hype those little scooters
that will keep you moving, even go to Hooters
if you're so inclined. I wouldn't mind.

So better not inquire how much time elapses
between electric charges and synapses;
just tell the stories of your early youth,
who cares if truth gets muddled in the mists of time

or if you leave the water running or the oven on . . . .
Just think how much they'll miss all that excitement when
you're gone.

In the Interval

In the interval between awake/asleep
The wishful thought takes hold and flourishes.
A good dream nourishes the weary, yes,
But wait!
It's far too late to dream of great successes.
Time to put away the pretty party dresses. Time
To mend the shroud,
pierced by longing, in a thousand places.
Time to inventory all the frowning faces.
Perhaps it's rash to throw my piles of paper in the trash.
Perhaps there's something brilliant that I said
In the interval between alive and dead.

Autumn

No use to tip the dealer
He just smiles. His job to deal the cards
is not in danger as long as strangers pay to play.
The sun shafts sideways on the mountain
shading autumn into winter.
Cats stay in, sleeping hearthside
as the wind unwinds the leaves from branches
and we pack in for the evening. Habitude makes it all right
but still I wish that it were morning, springtime, starting
over
Instead of ending, winter, and eternal night.

My health is failing
with a big
F

and I can't make it up by staying after school writing
"I will not get old"
on that big cosmic blackboard in the sky.

Bon Voyage

It wasn't easy, getting here
There were all those forms to fill out
taking off my shoes, showing my intent
and worst of all, selecting the right soul. I was never good
at making hard decisions but
finally I did embark down the birth canal, emerging
to the sound of Muzak, metallic clinking and all that light!
But I got it right; the trip
was worth the fee and I even became conduit
to other travelers who turned out well
despite their mode of transportation. I wonder
if the sundry souls who hunger for the journey knew
just what awaits them beyond their choices
would they clamor so for passage, to be borne
along this route of violence and beauty
to finally be stamped and folded in a passport full of riches
and regrets.

To Beloved Phil

It isn't convenient to die on a Friday:
The week-end all planned now has got to be scuttled
In favor of mourning and scrambling together
Memorial service and coffin and prayer.

When would it be better; to leave your shift early
And miss clocking out at the usual hour?
When would it be better; to race to the finish
Only to find that you got there too soon?

The glasses we raise in the pub on the corner
Lack substance, lack subtlety, verisimilitude,
Any remembrance, resemblance of you.
The stories we tell are a pale imitation
Of who we once knew, the astutest of gents.
It isn't convenient to die on a Friday,
It should have been many more, countless years hence.

Luncheon Manifesto

Don't let me die yet. I'm not finished
Somewhat diminished maybe, but not gone
My shrinking frame still carries on
About the weather and the politics
The dirty tricks that nature plays
And people, too. Oh, it's a zoo all right
But carnivals are basically carnivorous
We eat our own. Reason has flown
Away with expedient dismay
For who can witness this abysmal play
Of circumstances and not want to just give up?
I will not sup at tables that are so uncool
I'll play the fool and argue still
And try to bend your understanding to my will
Or failing that, just say farewell
Until we meet again in hell
Or someplace where they don't burn books
Or give you nasty looks for being who you are.
I'll send you salutations from afar
And wish you Darwin speed, good fortune and bonne
chance
Until we can resume our dance.

Extremities

My toes, shaped like Hebrew letters,
Unfettered by rabbinical restraint,
Resplendent in peach polish, frolic
In their gladiator sandals.
Would that my fingers could do likewise
But they cramp from overuse and age.
There are no nostrums that can straighten
Their intriguing curvature, nor cure
The spasms that pounce from nowhere
But their misshapen bends are graceful,
As if eternally in some balletic attitude
And I take pleasure in the thought
That they can never be surprised
In some ungainly pose.

Exalted as a malted

To a thirsty Jewish person from the Bronx
I think a drink
Of any kind would do except the hemlock
That was Socrates' undoing.
Was he ruing, at the moment of his quite heroic death,
The foolhardiness of trying to impress the logic of his
thinking
On a multitude that would have rather taken that same time
to go on drinking?

An Act of Faith

If I pile
the detritus of my life
high enough
in front and behind me,
Then the Angel of Death
will not know where to find me.
Letters to the Editor
may be your bread and butter but
don't advise me to eliminate clutter.
You cannot impress me
with your organizational skills
when neatness kills.

Doctor's Appointment

Why be morbid.
There is plenty of time
To spill the beans before
I kick the bucket.
Secrets of the universe abound in dreams
and truths unveil themselves encryptically.
I am aware that shortly all will be revealed
But until then I still need to be healed.

Hussy

Who could have thought
This flirtatious heart could still beat
In my ancient frame?
Playful to the end (which is getting nearer)
Nothing could be dearer to me than death unless
Of course, it is a new beginning,
And the sweet illusion that I am winning.

I Can't Go Yet

I can't go yet, with my shoes untied
There are way too many things I haven't tried
I haven't tried hang gliding, or the river cruises,
I haven't gone to Lourdes, consulted muses,
Joined a drumming circle or done yoga in the nude:
I really just can't leave without some certitude!

I can't go yet, with my bed unmade.
I haven't danced in sunshine or in shade
I can't do twenty laps; indeed, my cat
Won't even sit in mine! Now what is that!!

I really am not done, so pass me by.
I promise I'll be ready on your second try:
I will have packed
I will have enough underwear
I will have silk pajamas and a dancing bear
I will remember laughter and renounce the tears
And be appropriately grateful for the passing years
I will go sweetly, silently and with a bow
But just not now!

When I Vanish

Old Father Time is winding me down
Down to the second aborning I came.
Ticking me down to the very beginning
So I should not mind when I vanish.

Old Mother Earth is glad that I came
Dancing on sand and the grasses she gave
Singing to winds and crying to rain
So I should not mind when I vanish.

I am at once infant, and infinite old
Gasping for breath at the top of the stair
Bending to drink of the liquefied air
Audience yawning and ceasing to care
So they should not mind when I vanish

A LITTLE
LEVITY

Writer's Block

The muse
Refuses, lying still
The mute enchantress thwarts my will
She hides behind her Gorgon's hair
Pretending she was never there
At all. But I know better.

Seductive
In seclusion, laughs
At my frustrated epitaph:
"Here lies my claim to fame, interred
Because the bitch won't say a word."

Every Passing Bug Wants to Give Me a Hug

My stamina needs bolstering like my sofa needs upholstering
And I seem to be acquainted with each extravagantly tainted germ.
I am infirm.
It's not that I'm depressed; I could always use some rest,
But this enforced prone position leads to cheerless malnutrition
And no matter what I do, even taking shots for flu
Doesn't seem to do the trick
I'm still sick!
If a doctor, on inspection, finds I have a bad infection,
His invariable selection of efficacious medication turns out wrong,
Hence my song:
More, a dirge to my mortality; the issue of morality doesn't really enter in
Likely not a grievous sin
Did me in.
Much more likely something spikely with multiple appendages and hair.
I don't care
If I'm doomed to have the heaves until the damn thing leaves.

Even TV ad cartoons depicting germs as cute buffoons
Don't placate me
If they await me.
If I simply can't pronounce it, all I want to do is trounce it
Send it hither whence it came
I don't need to know its name!

He Was a Good Egg

In truth, I was rotund; a veritable sphere
But not so fat as to be unattractive
To the opposite sex. In fact,
The ladies would parade before me
While pretending to be doing errands.
Yes, on the fateful day in question,
I was sitting atop a promontory
From which I could see them coming and going
(In their sheer summer dresses)
When one of superior form did catch my eye but seemed
To disappear from view. At once intrigued
I swiveled mightily to affect a better purchase
From which to ascertain her attributes
When suddenly a gust of wind (it must have been,
For why else would I have so lost my bearings,
Being blessed with perfect balance and a
Kinesthetic sense second to no one)
Came from no where and toppled me
Off my vantage point and into great tumult
And derision. Oh!
At first they laughed, but then on seeing me
Unable thence to rise they sent for horses,
Would you believe! Yes, the four legged kind
Who consulted, snorting, with each other
And subsequently called for servants. By then

It was too late for medical opinions
And I lay shattered on the pavement
Ruing my misfortune and my penchant
For observing with favor those lithe beings
Well proportioned and curvaceous
Who deliberately sauntered past me, just pretending
Not to notice my unfailing dedication.

(Ah, it was they t'were my undoing
E'en tho I was not actively pursuing
Let alone actually wooing)
As I lay there in the gutter, not one word did I utter
Casting blame. For it doesn't suit a gentleman to
cavil and complain
My reputation may remain intact but alas
I cannot say the same for the rest of me.
For those winsome wily wenches got the best of me.

There They Were

There they were!
in broad daylight looking for all the world like
ladies of the evening, pushing
shopping carts around the floor at Sam's Club
gleaming patent leather spike heels, legs
so long and black and bare
ending in abbreviated shorts
the pubic hair had nowhere left to curl by God
the girls did glisten as they sauntered up the aisle,
veritable islands of desire unto themselves!

Pendule

Dangling, like a thalidomidic third leg,
The penis, as appendage, is unenviable:
Fully flaccid, evoking pity;
When erect, sufficiently suffused
To support a wash cloth, or a hand towel
At the very least.
So unleash the beast, and let's play house, or doctor
And I'll proctor the examination
And he who gets a passing grade
Gets laid.

Steinway

I don't feel guilty anymore
It stands, three legged, on the floor
black and imposing, but no threat
I still might sit and play it, yet
The days the weeks the years go by
Don't even seem to want to try
And all those lessons, all for naught
And all that paper music bought
And exhortations, "Practice! Practice!"
Might as well be yelling at a cactus
Oh prickly me, contrary, too
For I will do what I will do
What I won't do is sit and play
Sometime perhaps, but not today.

Confessions of a Thespian

It must have happened years ago
Don't really know, but I can guess
That when I finally came out, the nurses
Yelled a hearty, "YES!, It's a girl!"
And I was bathed in silver light.
Now I might try, but can't escape the need
To have that light again, indeed, and did I mention
I still love to be the center of attention?

Astaire and the Bear

You could teach a bear to dance
But I wouldn't take the chance
Some think hirsute is cute
I tend to doubt it.

You could teach a bear to dance
But you'll be looked at quite askance
And they'll wonder why you try
To go about it.

You could teach a bear to dance
Even find some small romance
In the soulful, doleful
Grunts that he's emitting.

You could teach a bear to dance
Even dress him up in pants
But I fear you'll earn
A diminishing return from where I'm sitting.

You could teach a bear to dance
And be all the rage in France
Or for all the world to see
Do reality TV
But the truth is, he's a bear
And he really doesn't care
So I'd take my passion hence
To the mundane world of gents
And if asked to spend the night
At least he just might be polite

Message from my Computer

My "data bases are out of date"!
Too late to call the geeks
I am owed a new binary code
At the very least. It leaks
Encryptions and will not re-boot.
My server will not serve.
Is this what I deserve?

I shall not pass this way again
I'm picking up my ball point pen.

Overdue

Is it really so pernicious
To put off doing dirty dishes
Or using all my craft and guile
To plan to stay abed awhile?

The worm may squirm to its content
It doesn't have to pay the rent
It has no civic obligations
Or inter-wormular relations.

The only thing it might deplore
Are early birds, and on that score
I think that you and I agree
They've not a thing to fear from me!

Whither do I Wither?

Where can I begin? With sugar
And it's evil twin: oh, honey!
How I long for the sweet taste
But I make haste to clear my shelves
Before the Devil's elves come back
To juggle cookies, Cracker Jacks and custard pies
Before my poor beleaguered eyes.
They've strewn the gingers snaps to lead me home
And thence astray.
I wish I weighed the same today as yesterday.
At least not more. I do deplore
The diet I must follow. Even if I do lose weight,
The victory and my poor tummy both are hollow.

Adverse to Verse

Rhyming can be a curse. Of course
There are worse things that could happen to a person
But still, to feel you have no will,
Except to make each final syllable the same
Creates a feeling that you want to blame somebody
Other than yourself! Some impish elf
Is making you compose these sorry couplets
I suppose.

Presumption

Do I channel Dorothy Parker, Edward Lear, or Ogden Nash?
It would be rash to presume such a close affinity
To so illustrious a trinity.

I do, however, share a certain Weltanschauung
And if there's a German word for it, how can it be wrong?

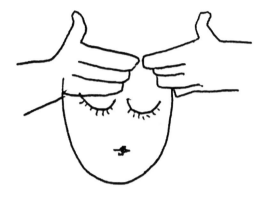

METAPHYSICAL
MUSINGS

The Spider

The tiny spider in the sink
Moves over so that I may wash my hands.
He understands I mean no harm
The charm is in the intention
Which I mention only in a passing way.
He needn't fear that he'll go down the drain today.

But yet, there is the problem of his getting wet.
Wouldn't he be better off inside a flower?
For if a shower then should suddenly appear
He need not fear, but simply hide under a leaf
But his belief, perhaps, in some big spider in the sky
Who watches over him and will not let him die
Is misplaced, for the god above is I.

And we, who make obeisance to the random gods,
What are the odds that anything will mitigate our fate?
Too late we find the drain is never far away,
No matter to which deities we pray.

Heaven is a Gated Community

Have you read the latest scientific article?
God turns out to be nothing more than a sub-atomic particle!
How's that for a disappointing denouement! I mean
Not only can he not be seen
He barely can be measured (let alone treasured)!
So no eye is on the sparrow
And even if I travel on the straight and narrow
I'll have a hard time with St. Peter at heaven's gate,
I'd better find another basis on which to negotiate.

If the Sky is Falling

If the sky is falling, after all,
It had to be the Skymaker who made it fall.
It would be odd
If God,
Having gone through all that trouble,
Finally reduced the world to rubble.
I'd wonder just to Whom
He is beholden to clean up His room.

Smiling

Smiling, I folded my assertions
And put them in the tip jar
What price mental health, I said
And waited for my change.

Assassins

The truth was for the taking
All those years of making scary faces
In the mirror to instill
That primal fear of self
Of animal brutality of innate evil
That resides in us in all of us just look
Into the mirror of your soul and weep
We are all doomed, my love,
Now go to sleep.

Merciless Moon

Merciless moon
We are captive
Under the glare of your flood light
Baring everything, revealing nothing, the world
Reduced to white and shades of black. Dormant
Evil prepares in shadows and will spring to life come morning.
I never thought I'd dread the dawn, but these
Are different days and foreboding stifles hope
Our feeble weapons lie quite shattered at our feet
and we are yours.
Why should I fear the moon
When darkest days await in fullest sunshine?
In fact, the moon may yet turn out to be
Our perfect friend. Only in its shadow side
Can we fall back, re-group and hide.

She's Gone

Unfathomable, she sank to mysterious depths
The only trace, the bubbles to the surface
Indicating where she was
Her company, the finless wonders of the deep
Deep chasms opened under her aggressive stroke
As she approached Olympic speeds
Across the bottom of the world
Amazingly engaged past old shipwrecks
And plundered spoils, past old mistakes and melancholies
Past the past and its seductive memories
The shoals of should have done
The reefs of madness.

Not once did she come up for air
Nor hesitate in treading water, dreading stillness
Driven by the odd compulsion to keep moving
Ever onward, blindly forward
For to stop would mean extinction.
Not this species
Not this time.
Her gills inflate
She flicks her tail.

She's gone.

A Piece of Your Brain the Size of a Grain of Sand Contains One Hundred Thousand Neurons, Two Million Axons, and One Billion Synapses

Can my tears wash them away?
Can my laughter multiply them?

We are walking games of chance
As likely to help a little old lady across the street
As to run her over with a steam shovel
And G-d
In His infinite wisdom and supply
Has seen fit to populate His universe
With such fly by nighters as could
Donate kidneys and deforest continents
Simultaneously.

Garbage

Whom can I trust to take the garbage out? Who
wise enough, or sane, who differentiates between the wheat
and chaff, can laugh while sorting through the muck
while waiting for the truck to take it all away?
What if it isn't even garbage day?

What if we're stuck with all the foul mistakes we made
While trading up? What if the trade was spurious?
I'm just curious.

Can sub-atomic particles give us another chance?
Is there room to re-arrange the molecules and dance
To an ineffable gavotte?
I guess not.

Of Course

Self pity isn't pretty
Like wallowing in unwashed underwear
Like stale aberrant odors
Like imminent decline, but it is mine.
I own the thing, the hiccup in the breath
The death of hope, the flat uncaring glance
That chances on the object of remorse
Of course I would change course
But I'm too sorry to
Of course.

Fatal Appointment
With a Squirrel

What ambition propelled him,
bounding graceful arcs of grey
across my path, as I
in my steel clad chariot
was pursuing mine?

Motherhood

Lullabies and laughter mask the moment
When the sacrifice is made
When the altar runs with blood
And my pulsing heart is torn out, eaten
With a little sacramental wine
When future howling generations
Sing the praises of the newest member of the tribe.

So crack my bones, I am dismembered
And my parts are fed to charity
Make a stew of my ambition. I am done.
I serve the greater Goddess of survival
The flesh of destiny the birth of all
Who came before and who will be again
Revolving in the chain of resurrected life
Devoured by my progeny I die to live forever.

False Profit

Practicing without a license
The charlatan pretended to treat
My broken soul with poultices;
Anodynes designed to rot my flesh internally.
I'd never know that it was gone until it went
Hell bent, into the firmament
And what is left is free, for all eternity
To seek some justice, or at least
A finders' fee.

Philosophic Theosophy

If I think about it I will find
That everything's a state of mind
(life being an illusion)
I have no confusion on that score
I may deplore the circumstances
But even if I take my chances
Chances are it all will just come out the way it will
I've had my fill of wringing hands
The Dalai Lama understands.

Secular Humanists

We are not virtuous because Daddy with a long white beard
is standing behind us with threats and incantations.
Our human relations don't depend on ritual and threats of
holy hell, and maybe it is just as well
that empathy does not derive from anything more distant
than our pre frontal lobe.
The sufferings of Job may be noteworthy but not relevant
to our human condition,
Extraordinary rendition being as foreign to our bodies,
as are the countries to which we send them,
So don't look to some old guy in the sky to mend them.
Dogma is a harder pill to swallow, and the rewards are
hollow,
If, after that, you can still go out and kick your cat.

TRUE
LOVE

True Love

Alternatively, there was the road not taken
The beau insulted, the book unread.
The other way forgotten, the narrow corridor
The only path not chosen by the conscious mind
But blind to possibilities I went the only way I could
And found you, hiding in the universe.

Shape Shifter

Shape shifter,
Benign presence, silent partner
In the corporation of my life.
How did I ever navigate without you?

I sank into soft autumn leaves,
Enveloped in the gold and warmth. A dream
I had when I was little,
Never finding that sense of joy again
Until today.
With you.
My love.

I Don't Think So

Give me a certainty
Give me a mountain to climb whose valley
Is lush with the fruits of my labor

Show me a plenitude
Show me the affluence earned
By a lifetime of poverty

Sing me a lullaby
Sing me a song with a melody
Old as my mother and sweet as her touch

Give me a certainty
That when I die
I won't miss you so much.

Lost

I dreamed of gilded buildings but
the streets slanted away from memory and
I was lost in architecture, a cross between
Potemkin's Village and the Imperial City
no way home to you.
And then I woke
and all the scary splendour of the irradiated city
became concentrated in your healing touch.
Your body nestled me and
I was saved.

Requiem

We shall not mingle ashes, no.
Styles of interment come and go
Not outer space, nor even vaults
Shall witness our eternal waltz
Ever green, recycled, we
May still be keeping company
Perhaps not shooting with the stars,
Just resting in adjacent jars.

Edwards Brothers Malloy
Thorofare, NJ USA
January 2, 2013